CLEVELAND BROWNS

MATT SCHEFF

WWW.APEXEDITIONS.COM

Copyright © 2025 by Apex Editions, Mendota Heights, MN 55120. All rights reserved. No part of this book may be reproduced or utilized in any form or by any means without written permission from the publisher.

Apex is distributed by North Star Editions:
sales@northstareditions.com | 888-417-0195

Produced for Apex by Red Line Editorial.

Photographs ©: Joe Robbins/AP Images, cover, 1; Kirk Irwin/AP Images, 4–5, 58–59; Frank Jansky/Icon Sportswire, 6–7; Bettmann/Getty Images, 8–9, 10–11; Robert Riger/Getty Images Sport/Getty Images, 12–13; Focus on Sport/Getty Images Sport/Getty Images, 14–15; Paul Spinelli/NFL Photos/AP Images, 16–17; Vic Stein/Getty Images Sport/Getty Images, 19; AP Images, 20–21, 22–23; Ronald C. Modra/Getty Images Sport/Getty Images, 24–25; George Gojkovich/Getty Images Sport/Getty Images, 26–27, 34–35; Tony Tomsic/AP Images, 29, 57; Mark Duncan/AP Images, 30–31; Donald Miralle/Allsport/Getty Images Sport/Getty Images, 32–33; Perry Knotts/AP Images, 36–37; Peter G. Aiken/Getty Images Sport/Getty Images, 38–39; Andy Lyons/Getty Images Sport/Getty Images, 40–41; Jason Miller/Getty Images Sport/Getty Images, 42–43, 44–45; Gregory Shamus/Getty Images Sport/Getty Images, 47, 54–55; iStockphoto, 48–49; Scott Boehm/AP Images, 50–51; Angelo Merendino/Corbis Sport/Getty Images, 52–53

Library of Congress Control Number: 2023921989

ISBN
979-8-89250-080-7 (hardcover)
979-8-89250-097-5 (paperback)
979-8-89250-130-9 (ebook pdf)
979-8-89250-114-9 (hosted ebook)

Printed in the United States of America
Mankato, MN
082024

NOTE TO PARENTS AND EDUCATORS

Apex books are designed to build literacy skills in striving readers. Exciting, high-interest content attracts and holds readers' attention. The text is carefully leveled to allow students to achieve success quickly.

TABLE OF CONTENTS

CHAPTER 1
DAWG POUND 4

CHAPTER 2
EARLY HISTORY 8

PLAYER SPOTLIGHT
OTTO GRAHAM 18

CHAPTER 3
LEGENDS 20

PLAYER SPOTLIGHT
JIM BROWN 28

CHAPTER 4
RECENT HISTORY 30

CHAPTER 5
MODERN STARS 38

PLAYER SPOTLIGHT
MYLES GARRETT 46

CHAPTER 6
TEAM TRIVIA 48

TEAM RECORDS • 56
TIMELINE • 58
COMPREHENSION QUESTIONS • 60
GLOSSARY • 62
TO LEARN MORE • 63
ABOUT THE AUTHOR • 63
INDEX • 64

CHAPTER 1

DAWG POUND

Cleveland Browns fans rise to their feet. The stadium is filled with brown and orange. The cheering grows louder and louder. The Browns defense needs a big play.

Cleveland Browns Stadium holds more than 67,000 fans.

The opposing quarterback takes the snap. Browns defenders crash through the line. Defensive end Myles Garrett blows past his blocker. He grabs the quarterback and throws him to the ground. It's a sack! The Browns are on a roll. The fans love it.

THE POUND

The Browns are famous for the Dawg Pound. This area is behind the stadium's east end zone. The fans there are known for being rowdy. Some dress up like dogs. After big plays, they chant, "Woof, woof, woof!"

Myles Garrett (95) celebrates a sack during a 2023 game against the Pittsburgh Steelers.

CHAPTER 2

EARLY HISTORY

The Cleveland Browns began play in 1946. They were part of a new league. It was called the AAFC. The Browns were the league's best team. They won four straight titles. However, the AAFC went out of business after the 1949 season.

Marion Motley (76) drags a defender during a 1947 game against the New York Yankees.

In 1950, the Browns joined the NFL. And they kept up their winning ways. The Browns reached the NFL title game seven times in the 1950s. They won three of them.

WHY THE BROWNS?

Cleveland fans voted on the team's name. It was named after Paul Brown. He helped start the team. He was also the team's first head coach.

Head coach Paul Brown (center) helped Cleveland win seven championships between 1946 and 1955.

The Browns had a few average years in the early 1960s. But before long, they were back on top. Cleveland won the NFL title game in 1964. The Browns crushed the Baltimore Colts 27–0. It was Cleveland's fourth NFL title.

A NEW ERA

The AFL began play in 1960. This league was separate from the NFL. But in 1970, the two leagues joined together. The NFL now had two conferences. The Browns became part of the American Football Conference (AFC).

Cleveland running back Jim Brown carries the ball during the 1964 NFL title game.

Bernie Kosar threw for more than 21,000 yards during his nine years with the Browns.

The Browns had some tough seasons in the 1970s and early 1980s. But things improved in 1985. That year, Cleveland drafted quarterback Bernie Kosar. He led the Browns to the AFC title game three times. However, Cleveland lost all three.

THE DRIVE

Cleveland led the Denver Broncos 20–13 late in the 1986 AFC title game. But Denver quarterback John Elway led a 98-yard drive to tie the game. Then Denver kicked a field goal in overtime to win. Football fans remember "The Drive" as one of the greatest moments in NFL history. But Browns fans remember it as one of the most painful.

In 1995, Browns owner Art Modell said he was moving the team to Baltimore. Browns fans were very angry. The NFL agreed to let Modell move the team. However, the Browns name stayed in Cleveland. So did the team's history. Modell's team became the Ravens. The Cleveland Browns returned to the NFL in 1999. But the team had new players and new coaches.

Browns fans displayed signs to show their anger at the team's owner.

PLAYER SPOTLIGHT

OTTO GRAHAM

Otto Graham didn't dream of being an NFL quarterback. He went to Northwestern University to play basketball. But the school's football coaches saw how athletic he was. They convinced him to join the team.

Graham was a natural. He could run and throw. When the Browns began play in 1946, head coach Paul Brown chose Graham as his quarterback. Graham played for 10 seasons. In that time, he led Cleveland to 10 straight title games. Graham was named the NFL's Most Valuable Player (MVP) three times.

OTTO GRAHAM THREW FOR MORE THAN 23,500 YARDS DURING HIS CAREER.

CHAPTER 3

LEGENDS

Otto Graham was the heart of the Browns in the 1940s and 1950s. But he wasn't alone. Marion Motley played running back and linebacker. He was one of the first Black players in pro football. Motley's hard-hitting style helped him run over tacklers. Dante Lavelli was a sure-handed receiver. He also played defensive end.

Marion Motley (76) led the NFL in rushing yards in the 1950 season.

LEADING THE WAY

Jim Brown was one of the greatest running backs of all time. A strong offensive line led the way for him. Gene Hickerson and Dick Schafrath helped make Cleveland's running game one of the best in the NFL.

Lou Groza spent 21 seasons with the Browns. He played offense and defense. He was also one of the NFL's best kickers. Paul Warfield was one of the league's best wide receivers. He averaged more than 20 yards per catch over his career.

Lou Groza (76) kicks an extra point during a 1952 game against the Philadelphia Eagles.

The Browns had an exciting offense in the late 1970s and early 1980s. Quarterback Brian Sipe was known for his strong arm. In 1980, he won the league's MVP Award. Running back Greg Pruitt was a strong runner and excellent receiver. Tight end Ozzie Newsome was one of the best pass catchers in the NFL.

THE KARDIAC KIDS

Browns fans called the 1979 and 1980 teams the Kardiac Kids. The team had a habit of playing heart-stopping games. They won most of them. Several came on thrilling, last-second scores.

Brian Sipe tossed 154 touchdown passes during his 10-year NFL career.

Clay Matthews Jr. made the Pro Bowl four times during his 16 years with the Browns.

Right guard Joe DeLamielleure was the heart of the Browns offense in the early 1980s. His blocking helped both the running game and the passing game. Bernie Kosar was a strong, accurate quarterback. He tossed 116 touchdown passes during his nine years with the team.

FOOTBALL FAMILY

Linebacker Clay Matthews Jr. is Cleveland's all-time leader in tackles. Matthews came from a football family. His father, Clay Matthews Sr., played in the NFL. So did his brother Bruce. And his son Clay Matthews III was one of the NFL's best linebackers of the 2010s.

PLAYER SPOTLIGHT

JIM BROWN

Jim Brown was a powerful runner. He was also a skilled pass catcher. Every time he touched the ball, he was a threat to score. Sometimes he would spin out of tackles. Other times he would simply run over defenders.

Brown played just nine seasons. In eight of those seasons, he led the league in rushing yards. Brown's final season came in 1965. That year, he won his third MVP Award. Then he shocked fans by retiring. Many football fans consider Brown the best running back in NFL history.

> **JIM BROWN TOPPED 1,200 RUSHING YARDS IN SEVEN OF HIS NINE SEASONS.**

CHAPTER 4

RECENT HISTORY

The Browns returned in 1999. Cleveland fans were thrilled to cheer on their team again. But the Browns struggled. They went 2–14 in 1999. The next year wasn't much better. In 2000, the Browns won only three games.

Browns players run onto the field for the team's first home game of the 1999 season.

Things started to look brighter in 2002. Quarterback Tim Couch led the Browns back to the playoffs. They faced the Pittsburgh Steelers. Cleveland led by 12 in the fourth quarter. But the Steelers came back to win 36–33.

Tim Couch led 11 game-winning drives in his five NFL seasons.

The loss to the Steelers marked the beginning of a tough time for Browns fans. The team went 17 straight seasons without making the playoffs. The team went through many quarterbacks and head coaches. In the 2010s, the Browns didn't have a single winning season.

FROM BAD TO WORSE

In 2016, the Browns went 1–15. Yet somehow, things got worse. In 2017, the Browns didn't win a single game. They joined the 2008 Detroit Lions as the only teams to go 0–16 in a season.

Center Alex Mack (55) was one of Cleveland's best players in the 2010s.

Wide receiver Jarvis Landry dives for a touchdown during Cleveland's playoff win over Pittsburgh.

In 2020, the Browns hired head coach Kevin Stefanski. He helped turn the team around. The Browns went 11–5 that season. They also ended their long playoff drought. Cleveland faced the Steelers in the playoffs. The Browns scored four touchdowns in the first quarter. They went on to win 48–37. It was Cleveland's first playoff victory since 1994.

BITTER RIVALS

The Browns have heated rivalries with the Steelers and the Cincinnati Bengals. But their biggest rival is the Baltimore Ravens. Many Browns fans haven't forgiven Baltimore for taking their team in the 1990s.

CHAPTER 5

MODERN STARS

Left tackle Joe Thomas was one of the best linemen in the NFL for more than a decade. Thomas was a powerful pass blocker. He also cleared the way for running backs. From 2007 to 2016, Thomas made the Pro Bowl 10 years in a row. He was voted into the Pro Football Hall of Fame in 2023.

Between 2007 and 2016, Joe Thomas was on the field for every Browns offensive play.

Braylon Edwards scored 28 touchdowns in his first four seasons with the Browns.

During the 2000s, Braylon Edwards was one of the fastest receivers in the NFL. His best season came in 2007. Edwards had 1,289 receiving yards. He also scored 16 touchdowns.

DEFENSIVE STAR

Joe Haden was a shutdown cornerback for the Browns. He was smart and athletic. Opposing quarterbacks always threw carefully when they sent the ball his way.

Baker Mayfield threw for more than 3,000 yards in each of his four seasons with Cleveland.

The Browns chose Baker Mayfield with the first pick in the 2018 draft. The quarterback threw 27 touchdown passes as a rookie. Then, in 2020, he led the team to a playoff win. One of Cleveland's best blockers was guard Joel Bitonio. He went to the Pro Bowl six years in a row from 2018 to 2023.

RETURN MAN

Josh Cribbs was one of the NFL's most dangerous returners in the 2000s. He scored 11 return touchdowns. His best season came in 2009. That year, Cribbs scored on three kickoff returns and one punt return.

The Browns chose Nick Chubb in the 2018 draft. Chubb quickly became one of the league's best running backs. He was also a great pass catcher. Chubb's speed and power made him hard to stop. Wide receiver Amari Cooper joined the Browns in 2022. His great hands helped him make highlight-reel catches.

Between 2018 and 2023, Nick Chubb had 60 runs of 20 or more yards.

PLAYER SPOTLIGHT

MYLES GARRETT

Defensive end Myles Garrett is a nightmare for quarterbacks. He's a big, powerful pass rusher. But he's also quick. Garrett can burst off the line in a heartbeat. Offenses usually double-team him. When they don't, Garrett often makes them pay.

Garrett is a sack expert. He brought down the quarterback 16 times in 2021. He recorded the same number the next year. In 2023, Garrett had one of his best seasons yet. He won the Defensive Player of the Year Award.

> **MYLES GARRETT AVERAGED MORE THAN 12 SACKS PER YEAR IN HIS FIRST SEVEN SEASONS.**

47

CHAPTER 6

TEAM TRIVIA

The Browns play in Cleveland Browns Stadium. Construction on the stadium began in 1997. The Browns didn't have a team that year. But the stadium was ready when the team restarted in 1999. The stadium lies along the shore of Lake Erie.

The Browns' stadium is in downtown Cleveland, Ohio.

Browns fans have been through a lot. They lost their team for three years. They dealt with many seasons of losing football. But they are some of the most loyal fans in the NFL. They keep showing up whether the team is winning or losing.

BROWNIE THE ELF

Brownie the Elf is Cleveland's mascot. Brownies are mythical creatures. They are known for causing trouble. Many fans love Brownie. But others blame him for the team's bad luck.

Some Browns fans show their support by wearing dog masks.

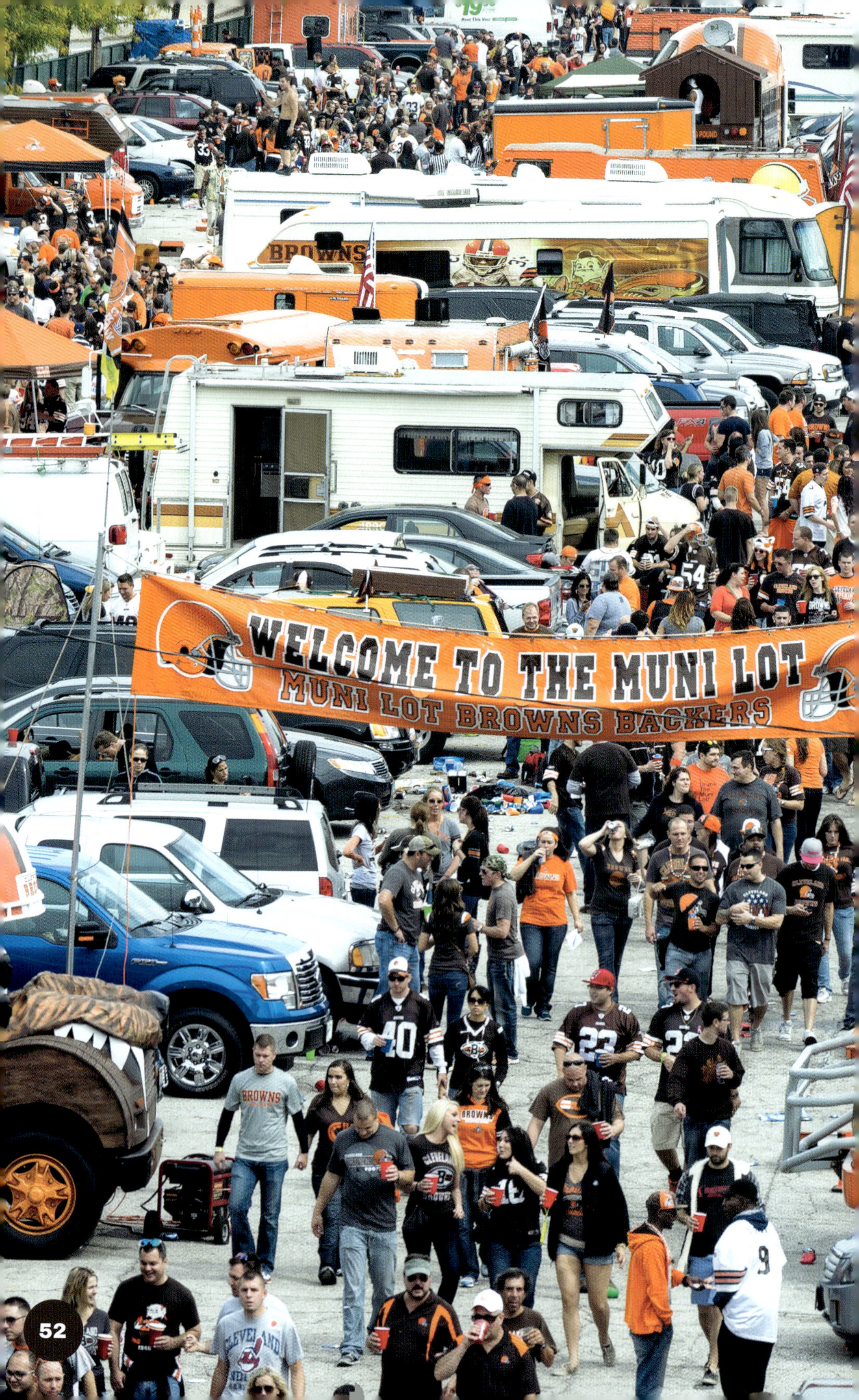
WELCOME TO THE MUNI LOT
MUNI LOT BROWNS BACKERS
BROWNS

Tailgating before home games is a tradition for many Browns fans. They gather in parking lots hours before kickoff. They play music and games. They cook food. And they pump themselves up for the game.

Many Browns fans arrive early to have fun in the parking lots near the stadium.

The Browns sport all-white uniforms during a 2023 game against the San Francisco 49ers.

The Browns are the only NFL team without a logo on their helmets. The team has changed its uniform design several times over the years. But the team's colors have remained the same. They are brown, orange, and white.

TEAM RECORDS

All-Time Passing Yards: 23,713
Brian Sipe (1974–83)

All-Time Touchdown Passes: 174
Otto Graham (1946–55)

All-Time Rushing Yards: 12,312
Jim Brown (1957–65)

All-Time Receiving Yards: 7,980
Ozzie Newsome (1978–90)

All-Time Interceptions: 45
Thom Darden (1972–81)

All-Time Sacks: 88.5
Myles Garrett (2017–)

All-Time Scoring: 1,608
Lou Groza (1946–67)

All-Time Coaching Wins: 158
Paul Brown (1946–62)

AAFC Titles: 4
(1946, 1947, 1948, 1949)

NFL Titles: 4
(1950, 1954, 1955, 1964)

All statistics are accurate through 2023.

57

TIMELINE

1946 — The Browns win the first AAFC title. They go on to win three more before the league goes out of business after the 1949 season.

1950 — The Browns join the NFL and win the league's championship in their first season.

1955 — The Browns go to their 10th straight championship game and defeat the Los Angeles Rams.

1964 — Jim Brown leads Cleveland to its fourth NFL title.

1986 — The Browns reach the AFC title game, but they lose to Denver.

1996
Owner Art Modell takes his team to Baltimore. Cleveland is left without a team.

1999
The Browns return to the NFL, playing in the new Cleveland Browns Stadium.

2017
The Browns become just the second team to go 0–16 in a season.

2020
New head coach Kevin Stefanski leads the Browns to their first playoff win since 1994.

2023
Defensive end Myles Garrett is named Defensive Player of the Year.

COMPREHENSION QUESTIONS

Write your answers on a separate piece of paper.

1. Write a paragraph that explains the main ideas of Chapter 2.

2. Who do you think was the greatest player in Browns history? Why?

3. Which player led the Browns to 10 straight title games from 1946 to 1955?
    - **A.** Jim Brown
    - **B.** Otto Graham
    - **C.** Brian Sipe

4. Why do many Browns fans consider the Ravens their biggest rival?
    - **A.** Cleveland and Baltimore are very close to each other.
    - **B.** The two teams have been playing each other for nearly 100 years.
    - **C.** Browns fans blame Baltimore for taking their team in the 1990s.

5. What does **rowdy** mean in this book?

*The fans there are known for being **rowdy**. Some dress up like dogs. After big plays, they chant, "Woof, woof, woof!"*

    A. quiet, dull, and bored
    B. smart, funny, and polite
    C. loud, wild, and excited

6. What does **drought** mean in this book?

*He helped turn the team around. The Browns went 11–5 that season. They also ended their long playoff **drought**.*

    A. a long period without success
    B. a long period with great success
    C. a long period with the same players

Answer key on page 64.

GLOSSARY

conferences
Groups of teams that make up a sports league.

drafted
Selected a new player coming into the league.

playoffs
A set of games played after the regular season to decide which team is the champion.

retiring
Ending one's career.

rivalries
Ongoing competitions that bring out strong emotion from fans and players.

rookie
An athlete in his or her first year as a professional player.

sack
A play that happens when a defender tackles the quarterback before he can throw the ball.

snap
The start of each play when the center passes the ball back to the quarterback.

tailgating
Gathering in a parking lot before a game, usually with food.

tradition
A way of doing something that is passed down over many years.

TO LEARN MORE

BOOKS

Adamson, Thomas K. *The Cleveland Browns*. Minneapolis: Bellwether Media, 2024.

Coleman, Ted. *Cleveland Browns All-Time Greats*. Mendota Heights, MN: Press Box Books, 2022.

Doeden, Matt. *Football's Biggest Rivalries*. North Mankato, MN: Capstone Press, 2024.

ONLINE RESOURCES

Visit **www.apexeditions.com** to find links and resources related to this title.

ABOUT THE AUTHOR

Matt Scheff is an author and artist living in Alaska. He enjoys mountain climbing, fishing, and curling up with his two Siberian huskies to watch sports.

INDEX

Bitonio, Joel, 43
Brown, Jim, 22, 28
Brown, Paul, 10, 18

Chubb, Nick, 44
Cooper, Amari, 44
Couch, Tim, 32
Cribbs, Josh, 43

DeLamielleure, Joe, 27

Edwards, Braylon, 41

Garrett, Myles, 6, 46
Graham, Otto, 18, 20
Groza, Lou, 23

Haden, Joe, 41
Hickerson, Gene, 22

Kosar, Bernie, 15, 27

Lavelli, Dante, 20

Matthews, Clay, Jr., 27
Mayfield, Baker, 43
Modell, Art, 16
Motley, Marion, 20

Newsome, Ozzie, 24

Pruitt, Greg, 24

Schafrath, Dick, 22
Sipe, Brian, 24
Stefanski, Kevin, 37

Thomas, Joe, 38

Warfield, Paul, 23

ANSWER KEY:
1. Answers will vary; 2. Answers will vary; 3. B; 4. C; 5. C; 6. A